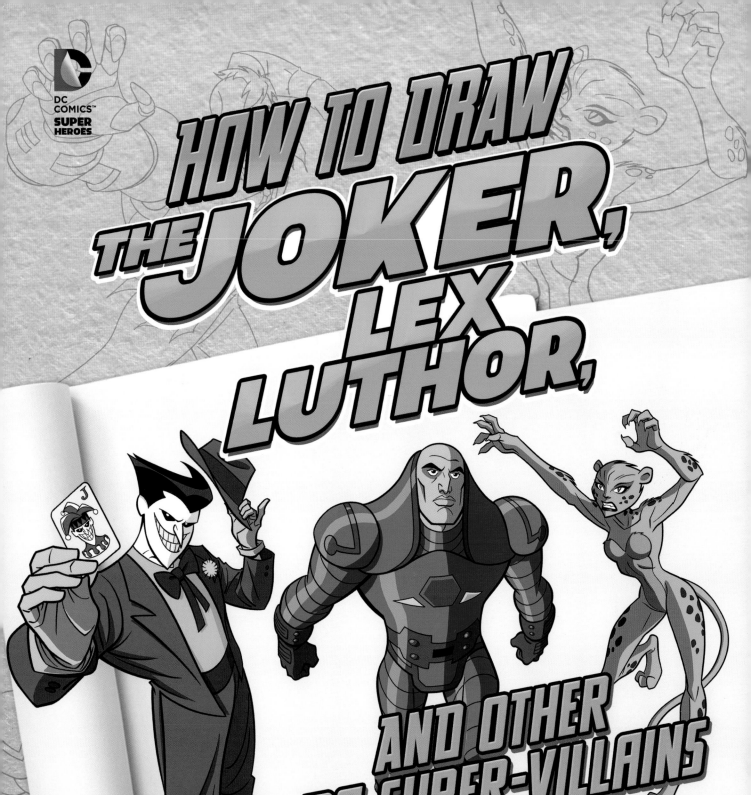

HOW TO DRAW THE JOKER, LEX LUTHOR, AND OTHER DC SUPER-VILLAINS

DC COMICS™
SUPER
HEROES

by Aaron Sautter
illustrated by Tim Levins

CAPSTONE PRESS
a capstone imprint

Published in 2015 by Capstone Press,
a Capstone Imprint
1710 Roe Crest Drive
North Mankato, Minnesota 56003
www.capstonepub.com

STAR33521

Library of Congress Cataloging-in-Publication Data
Sautter, Aaron.
How to draw the Joker, Lex Luthor, and other DC super-villains /
by Aaron Sautter, illustrated by Tim Levins.
pages cm.—(DC super heroes. Drawing DC super heroes)
Summary: "Simple step-by-step instructions teach readers how to draw Lex Luthor, the Joker, and several other DC super-villains"—Provided by publisher.
ISBN 978-1-4914-2155-0 (library binding)
1. Cartoon characters—Juvenile literature. 2. Supervillains in art—Juvenile literature.
3. Drawing—Technique—Juvenile literature. I. Levins, Tim. II. Title.
NC1764.8.V55S28 2015
741.5'1—dc23   2014023863

Credits:
Designer: Ted Williams
Art Director: Nathan Gassman
Production Specialist: Kathy McColley

Design Elements

Capstone Studio: Karon Dubke; Shutterstock: Artishok, Bennyartist, Eliks, gst, Mazzzur, Roobcio

Printed in the United States of America in North Mankato, Minnesota
092014   008482CGS15

DRAWING PROJECTS

LET'S DRAW DC SUPER-VILLAINS!

What would Superman or Batman do if they didn't need to stop Lex Luthor or the Joker? How would Wonder Woman spend her time if she didn't have to fight Cheetah? Everybody loves super heroes. But the truth is, without super-villains to fight against, super heroes wouldn't have much to do.

Every super hero has a Rogues Gallery of villains to fight. Just like heroes, super-villains have a variety of powers, special abilities, and backgrounds. Some are super-intelligent humans. Others are powerful aliens. Some villains devise evil plans to get revenge on their archenemies. Others simply want to take over and rule the world. But villains all have one thing in common—they give us a reason to cheer for our favorite super heroes!

Welcome to the world of DC super-villains! On the following pages you'll learn to draw several fearsome villains such as Sinestro, Cheetah, and Black Manta.

Unleash your imagination and see what happens when your favorite heroes clash with these sinister super-villains!

4

WHAT YOU'LL NEED

You don't need superpowers to draw menacing villains. But you'll need some basic tools. Gather the following supplies before starting your awesome art.

PAPER: You can get special drawing paper from art supply and hobby stores. But any type of blank, unlined paper will work fine.

PENCILS: Drawings should always be done in pencil first. Even the pros use them. If you make a mistake, it'll be easy to erase and redo it. Keep plenty of these essential drawing tools on hand.

PENCIL SHARPENER: To make clean lines, you need to keep your pencils sharp. Get a good pencil sharpener. You'll use it a lot.

ERASERS: As you draw, you're sure to make mistakes. Erasers give artists the power to turn back time and erase those mistakes. Get some high quality rubber or kneaded erasers. They'll last a lot longer than pencil erasers.

BLACK MARKER PENS: When your drawing is ready, trace over the final lines with black marker pen. The dark lines will help make your characters stand out on the page.

COLORED PENCILS AND MARKERS: Ready to finish your masterpiece? Bring your characters to life and give them some color with colored pencils or markers.

5

THE JOKER

Real Name: unknown

Home Base: Gotham City

Occupation: professional criminal

Enemy of: Batman

Abilities: above-average strength, genius-level intelligence, skills in chemistry and engineering

Background: Also known as the Clown Prince of Crime, the Joker is Batman's most dangerous enemy. When he fell into a vat of toxic waste, he was transformed into an evil madman. The chemicals bleached his skin white, dyed his hair green, and peeled his lips back into a permanent, hideous grin. The Joker delights in tormenting Batman and the innocent people of Gotham City.

DRAWING IDEA
Try drawing the Joker with a deadly hand buzzer or other practical joke device.

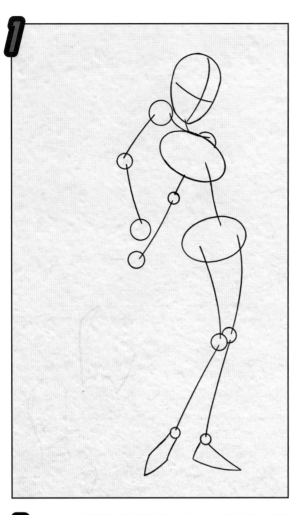

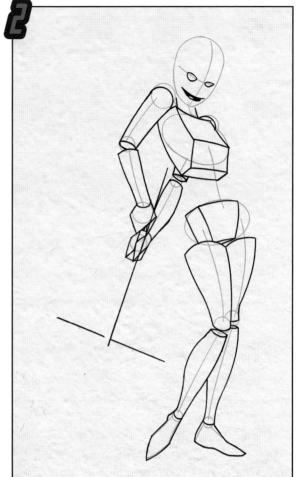

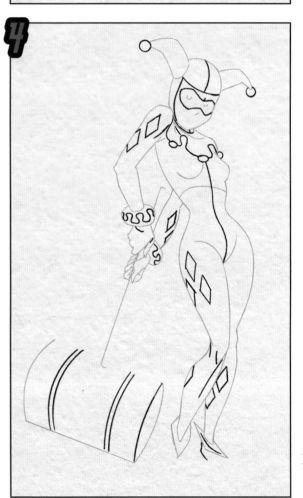

HARLEY QUINN

Real Name: Dr. Harleen Quinzel

Home Base: Gotham City

Occupation: psychiatrist, professional criminal

Enemy of: Batman

Abilities: Olympic-level gymnast and acrobat

Equipment: giant mallet

Background: Dr. Harleen Quinzel was once a successful psychiatrist at Gotham City's Arkham Asylum. But when she met the Joker, everything changed. When the Joker told Harley the heartbreaking, yet fake, story of his troubled childhood, her heart was won over. Harley fell in love with the Joker and soon helped him escape. She now clowns around Gotham City as Harley Quinn, the Joker's girlfriend and partner in crime.

DRAWING IDEA
Try drawing Harley and the Joker working together to set a deadly trap for Batman and Robin.

5

BANE

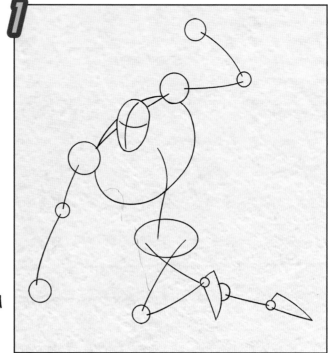

Real Name: unknown

Home Base: Gotham City

Occupation: assassin and professional criminal

Enemy of: Batman

Abilities: superhuman strength, genius-level intellect

Equipment: Venom drug

Background: Bane's background is a mystery, even to Batman. The only thing known for sure is that Bane was once a prisoner. He was chosen as a test subject for a new drug called Venom. The drug gave Bane superhuman strength. He now uses it to stay strong and works as one of Gotham City's criminal masterminds. Bane's greatest desire is to be the one person who can defeat the Dark Knight—permanently.

DRAWING IDEA
Try drawing Bane brawling with Batman on a bridge in Gotham City.

DRAWING IDEA

Next try drawing Catwoman working with Batman to stop Mr. Freeze's wicked plans!

CATWOMAN

Real Name: Selina Kyle

Home Base: Gotham City

Occupation: professional thief

Abilities: stealth, gymnastics, and martial arts skills

Equipment: retractable claws

Background: Selina Kyle became an orphan at a young age. She grew up committing petty crimes to survive on the streets. Now as Catwoman, Selina is an incredibly stealthy and skilled burglar. She preys on Gotham City's wealthy citizens while protecting the city's less fortunate people. Selina has helped Batman stop major criminals on several occasions. But their partnerships never last long. She has no interest in ending her own thieving ways.

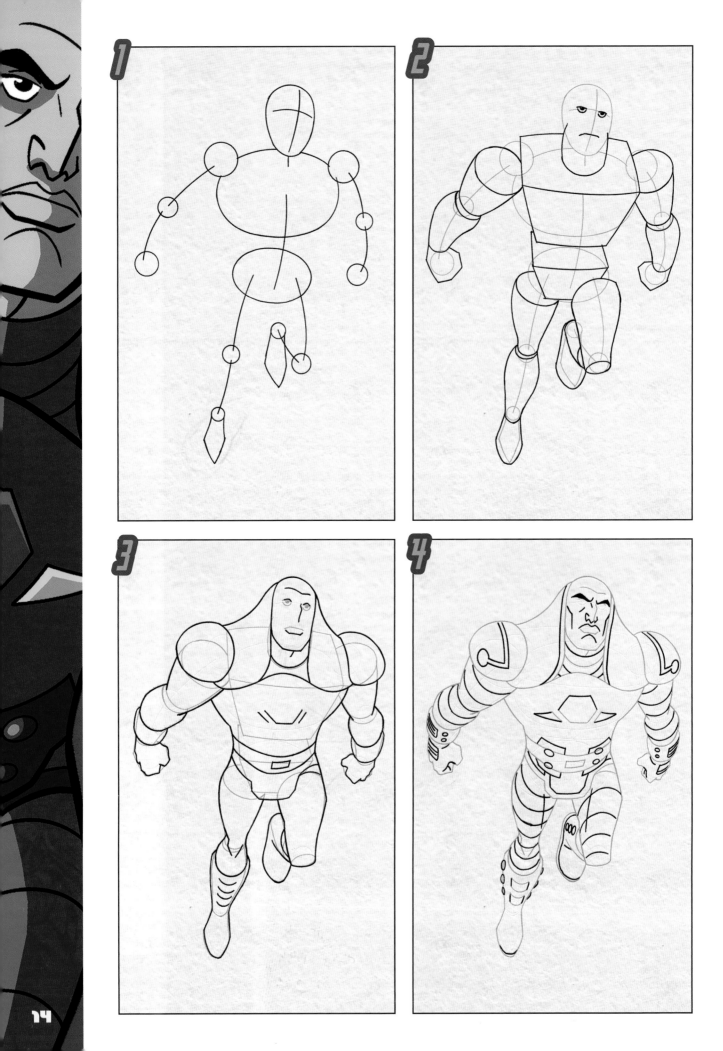

BATTLE ARMOR LEX

Real Name: Lex Luthor

Home Base: LexCorp, Metropolis

Occupation: successful businessman, criminal mastermind

Enemy of: Superman

Abilities: scientific genius

Equipment: Kryptonite battle suit

DRAWING IDEA
Try drawing Lex battling Superman in his armor high over Metropolis!

Background: Lex Luthor is one of Metropolis' richest and most powerful people. Behind the scenes he is a criminal mastermind and a scientific genius. To deal with Superman, Lex built a Kryptonite-powered battle suit. The armored suit gives him super-strength and allows him to fly. It's also armed with powerful Kryptonite energy weapons. While wearing his special battle suit, Lex is nearly a match for Superman.

METALLO

Real Name: John Corben

Home Base: Metropolis

Occupation: criminal and super-villain

Enemy of: Superman

Abilities: enhanced strength and speed, metal transformation

Background: John Corben was a criminal once employed by Lex Luthor. While in prison, Luthor infected Corben with a deadly disease. To save himself, Corben agreed to an experimental medical procedure. But when he woke, he discovered that his brain had been placed into a cyborg body powered by green Kryptonite. Now known as Metallo, he is nearly as strong and fast as Superman. The radiation from his Kryptonite heart can be lethal for the Man of Steel.

DRAWING IDEA
Try drawing Metallo using his Kryptonite powers in a face-off against the Man of Steel!

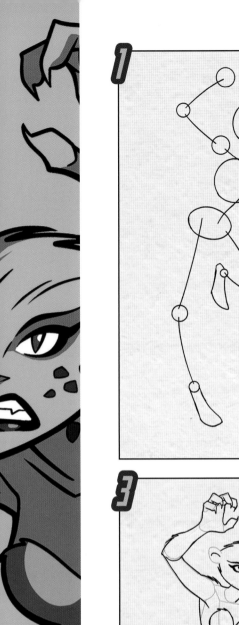

1

2

3

4

DRAWING IDEA
Now try drawing Cheetah fighting Wonder Woman with her catlike reflexes and razor-sharp claws!

CHEETAH

Real Name: Barbara Ann Minerva

Home Base: Nottingham, United Kingdom

Occupation: biologist, professional criminal

Enemy of: Wonder Woman

Abilities: catlike agility and reflexes, enhanced strength and speed, night vision, razor-sharp claws

Background: Dr. Barbara Ann Minerva was a biologist working on advanced genetics research. One day she decided to test her research on herself. But she was transformed into a half-human, half-cheetah hybrid. She was soon considered a freak by her fellow scientists and others. Cheetah then turned to a life of crime. She is cunning and clever, and her catlike abilities make her a dangerous foe for Wonder Woman.

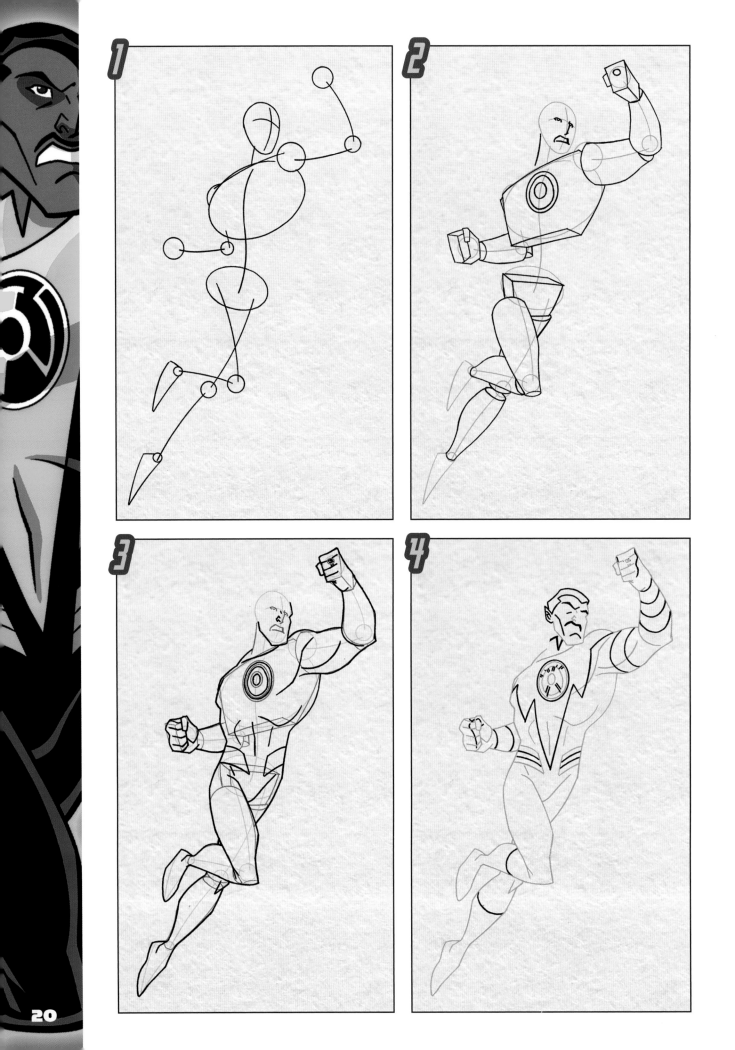

SINESTRO

Real Name: Thaal Sinestro

Home Base: Korugar, Qward

Occupation: Yellow Lantern

Enemy of: Green Lantern Corps

Abilities: military command, hand-to-hand combat skills, genius intellect

Equipment: yellow power ring

Background: Originally from the planet Korugar, Thaal Sinestro was once a famous member of the Green Lantern Corps. But he later turned evil and became a dictator over his home planet. Sinestro was eventually captured and banished to the planet Qward. However, he later obtained a yellow power ring that was just as powerful as the Lanterns' green rings. Sinestro then formed the Sinestro Corps and swore to get his revenge against the Green Lanterns.

DRAWING IDEA
Next try drawing Sinestro creating a powerful weapon with his yellow ring to fight Green Lantern!

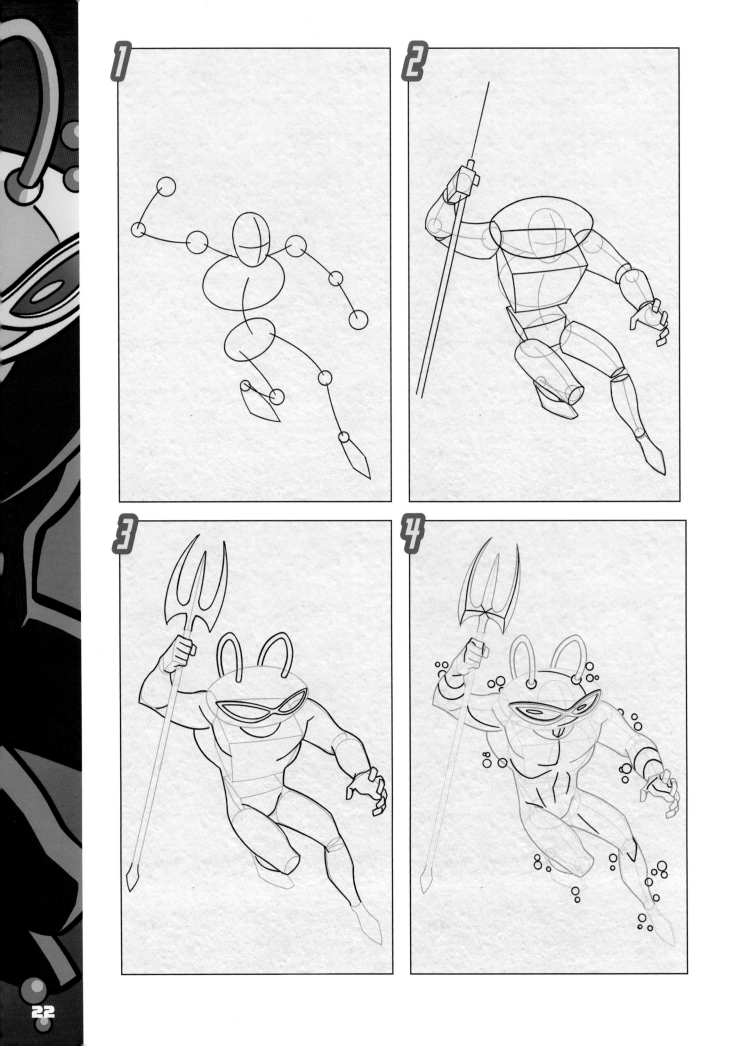

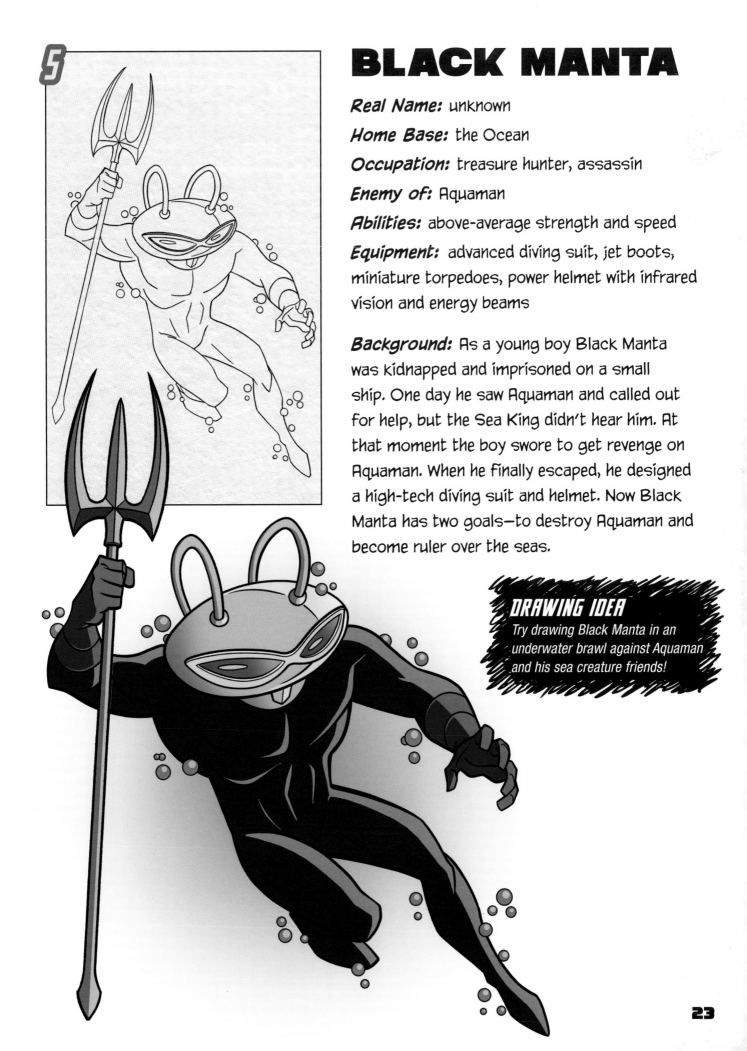

BLACK MANTA

Real Name: unknown

Home Base: the Ocean

Occupation: treasure hunter, assassin

Enemy of: Aquaman

Abilities: above-average strength and speed

Equipment: advanced diving suit, jet boots, miniature torpedoes, power helmet with infrared vision and energy beams

Background: As a young boy Black Manta was kidnapped and imprisoned on a small ship. One day he saw Aquaman and called out for help, but the Sea King didn't hear him. At that moment the boy swore to get revenge on Aquaman. When he finally escaped, he designed a high-tech diving suit and helmet. Now Black Manta has two goals—to destroy Aquaman and become ruler over the seas.

DRAWING IDEA
Try drawing Black Manta in an underwater brawl against Aquaman and his sea creature friends!

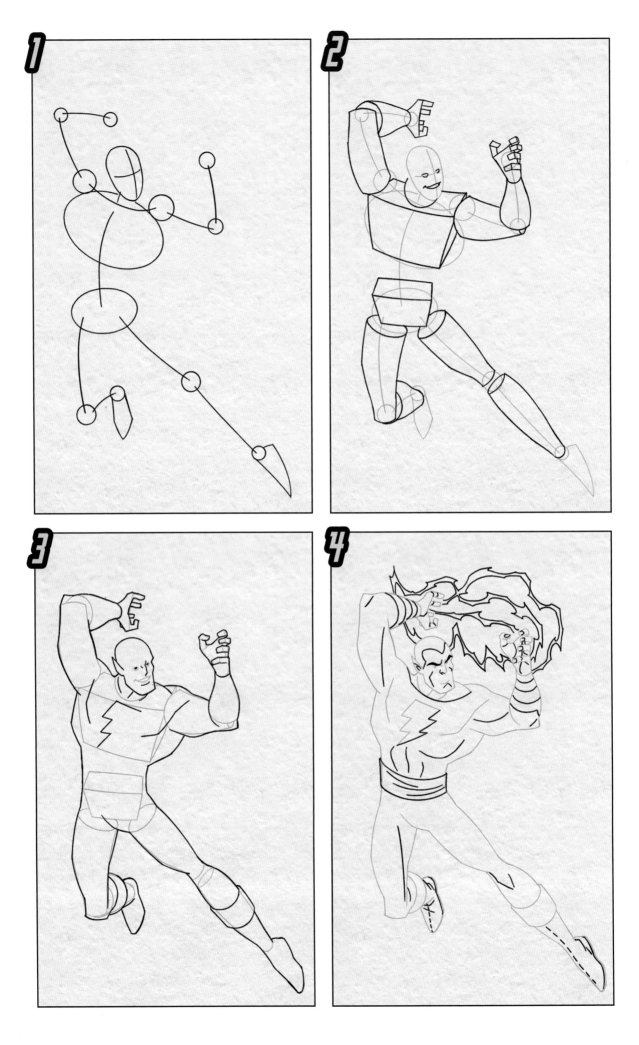

BLACK ADAM

Real Name: Teth-Adam

Home Base: Kahndaq

Occupation: dictator

Enemy of: SHAZAM!

Abilities: superhuman strength, speed, and stamina; enhanced intelligence; accelerated healing; flight; invulnerability

DRAWING IDEA
Try drawing Black Adam using his magical powers to battle his archenemy SHAZAM!

Background: Teth-Adam was once a fair and honest prince. The wizard Shazam! gave him the powers of the gods Shu, Heru, Amon, Zehuti, Aton, and Mehen. But Adam later became a cruel dictator. Eventually, the wizard trapped Adam's soul and powers in a magic necklace. However, the necklace was later discovered by Adam's descendant, Theo Adam. Now Black Adam's powers and memories live on through Theo. Only SHAZAM! can stop the super-villain's goal of ruling the world.

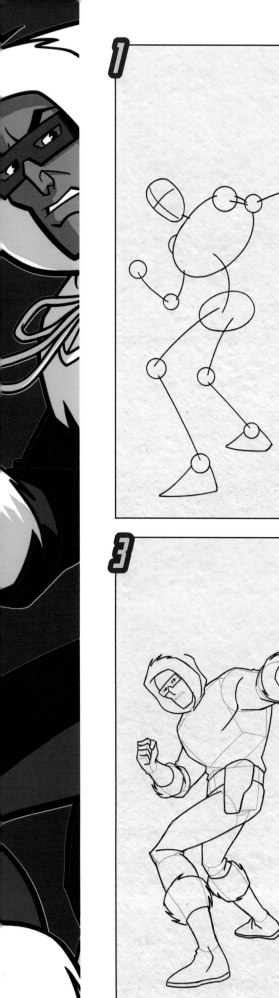

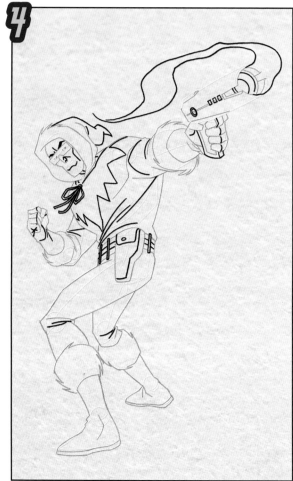

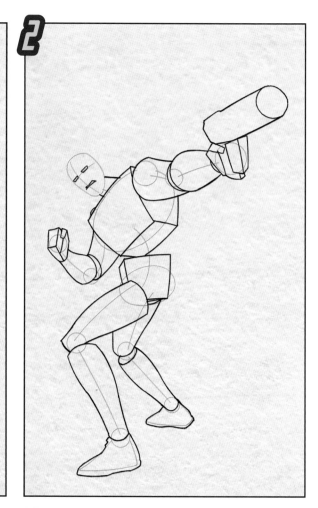

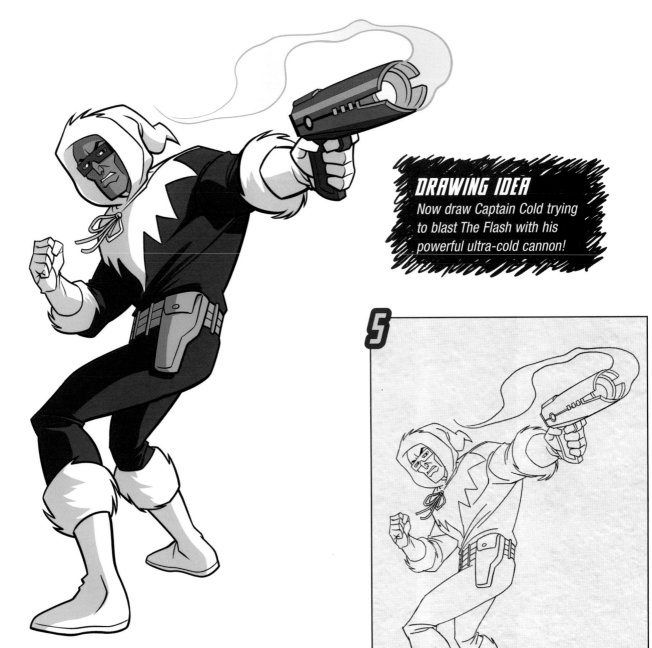

DRAWING IDEA
Now draw Captain Cold trying to blast The Flash with his powerful ultra-cold cannon!

CAPTAIN COLD

Real Name: Leonard Snart

Home Base: Central City

Occupation: professional criminal

Enemy of: The Flash

Abilities: skilled marksman, excellent strategist

Equipment: cold gun

Background: Captain Cold's name serves him well. He has nerves of ice and his cold heart helps him stay cool and collected in any situation. His special cold gun can instantly freeze objects into solid ice. Captain Cold also created an ultra-cold cannon that can bring even The Flash to a standstill. Now he looks for his chance to put the Scarlet Speedster on ice for good!

SUPER-VILLAINS UNITED

Super-villains usually like to work alone. However, being a successful criminal can be difficult with super heroes around. To get an advantage, villains sometimes form secret groups to fight their enemies together. These groups have gone by several names including the Secret Society of Super-Villains, the Injustice League, and the Legion of Doom. Villains can be powerful and dangerous when they team up. But luckily, villains have a fatal flaw—they usually don't work well together. They often end up fighting one another instead of the heroes they hate!

INTERNET SITES

FactHound offers a safe, fun way to find Internet sites related to this book.
All of the sites on FactHound have been researched by our staff.

Here's all you do:

Visit *www.facthound.com*

Type in this code: 9781491421550

Check out projects, games and lots more at
www.capstonekids.com

TITLES IN THIS SET

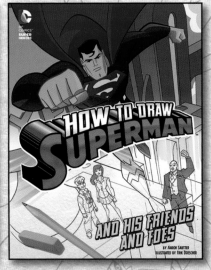

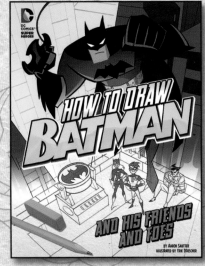

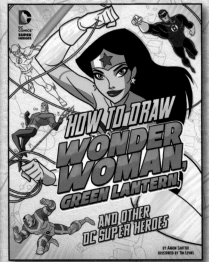